The Chains That Love

Broke

Becoming Free

———————

Kimberlee O

The Chains That Love Broke

Author: Kimberlee O

Published By

Faith Walk

Courageousfaithwalk.com

Printed in the United States

Copyright © 2014 by Kimberlee O

ISBN-13: 978-0615994819

ISBN-10:0615994814

Dedication

This book comes straight from my heart, revealing not only what it is like to go through what I am about to share, but also what it is like to come out victorious. God has already won the battle: He just waits for us to agree with Him. I dedicate this book to the God who has never left me. He has encouraged me, held me, and pushed me. I will always love my Kingdom Father.

To my beautiful children, Juma, Mykayla, and Mykeal, who has been my beacon to keep going – creating within me a no-quit attitude. They are everything to me, and I thank God for such precious gifts.

To everyone who has played a vital role in who I am today. Thank you! I am grateful for the deposits you all have made into my life.

You are all jewels.

To the person who changed my life forever; you taught me to dig just deeper. To the one whom God sent to set afire the passion inside -Thank you - I will be forever grateful.

Introduction

We all have at one time or another found ourselves trapped and in bondage to past failures, hurts, circumstances – enslaved way too long. Struggling with giving love and receiving love – all the while desperately longing to find some level of happiness in this life – without realizing that everything we need is right at our fingertips...

The beauty of life is that we already have within us the ability to create happiness, give love and be loved. We have been given power to break the chains that are designed to keep us in bondage -by suffocating our hopes, purpose, and zeal for life. I am here to tell you that each day that you get up and give it your best - you will not be disappointed or defeated. We all must carry our crosses - even with the blood, sweat and tears. You can make it, and not only make it: you can stand to tell the story of a renewed life and joy brand new. I am excited to bring you along on my journey of victory. My hope is that through this journey with me - you will see a God that swells my heart and makes me strong. It is within each of us – power unstoppable.

God has instilled greatness within us and sometimes it takes being broken for us to shine brighter. If we come out of our comfort zones and ways do doing thing, we will gain and understanding that God knows best. As you read, this I pray for peace and joy to fill you, and that you find within you the warrior that will not quit. Imagine that I am holding your hand and we are walking through this together. You will experience his supernatural blessings in your life from this day forward.

There is a champion within you - you are a child of the highest God. I hope that those who read this book see the victor in themselves. God blesses us despite our messes. He can remove the victim mentality from within you and cause you to step into the space of victory that was yours all along.

CONTENTS

Chapter One

Whose Are You?

It is liberating to embrace the fact that, first, you are a child of God - created in His image. This says that you are incredible and were designed to do, above all, incredible things. It does not matter who your parents are, if you are single, married or divorced: within your humanness is the spiritual, which is so much more powerful. Step outside of the limited framework of what makes you, you. It is true; you can't ignore the connections that are made throughout life that help to shape you, but what you *can* do is focus on the power rather than the lack of it. You can do and think great things - live a life God has already given you by the sacrifice of Jesus. Meditate on whose you are, and I assure you it will open doors that you never imagined would open. Whose are you?

The earliest memories of my childhood include watching a woman being beaten down by a man who I am sure she believed loved her. Somehow, she withstood his fits of drunkenness and fighting fits of rage. They came down upon her with such horror

1

that she somehow totally gave up and became his captured slave bound by alcohol abuse, fights, and disappointment. It was horrific as a small child to watch such tragedy befall her without any fighting will to remove herself from what seemed to drain any light she may have had in her life. As I stood next to my older siblings, a man straddled my mother - threatening to harm her. I recall hearing her shrill scream as she cried out that he was going make her lose the baby that she carried - it seemed time stood still. Even as young as I was, I hurt for her. She would later find her way out, only to leave us with our grandmother while she embarked upon

searching the world for what she would never find. My precious grandmother did what she felt necessary during a time when her daughter wandered aimlessly lost. She fed us and watched over us like we were her own. I promised myself that *I* would make it out - nothing would stop me. I remember later sleeping at a friend's house and being awakened and told that I had a phone call: my grandmother had passed. I shivered on the sofa, stifled cold with fear of what would happen next. On the night that I returned home from church, I was met by my mother who dropped my youngest brother off, demanding that we enter the house and go to sleep. I watched her drive off with a man who had no care or concern for the children she left behind. The world's idea of love certainly was not God's love. I paced back and forth across the floor, tiptoeing to not wake anyone – my heart thumping within the walls of my chest. I searched for anything that had any special meaning to me to carry along. I was getting myself out of this situation once and for all. I grabbed the diary that sported many bright colors on the cover, but within it lay some of my deepest, darkest thoughts. Like a thief in the night, I managed to sneak out with a church member, unnoticed by anyone in the home. I had no idea where I would end up. Truthfully, I should have been scared to death, but somewhere within - I trusted whose hands I was in.

I entered a foster home parented by a single hard-working woman. She had never married, but she gave birth to one child. She introduced me to a concept that was foreign to me: the success of a black woman. She worked hard, and she participated religiously in the Christian Science church. Through her I learned that God loves black people, too. (Tables do turn.) I longed to stay with my familiar church family, but I was told I had to remain where I was. I was told that a black child needed to see a black family who could provide a more positive example. This frustrated me so that I cried myself sick for a full day, and I woke in the middle of the night with my heart feeling like it was coming out of my chest. It was then that I had this conversation with myself: I could either make the best of this situation, or I could stress myself enough to make myself ill. From that point on, I accepted where I was, began to make friends in the neighborhood and participated in sports which I loved so much. One requirement made by the youth service that handled my foster care was that I had to attend counseling sessions. One evening as I was returning home from school – my Spanish teacher called the house to say she couldn't reach me, and that the always-good kid had sat in class all day with her head on the table – refusing to participate. There I was skipping happily home, and then the upbeat person that walked into the house was suddenly halted when I saw my foster mother and case worker sitting on the sofa.

Now, in the world of foster care that could mean one of many things: you may be moved to another home, you may be in trouble, etc. At that moment they told me that I had to attend counseling. I sat and looked at the case worker and my foster mother without saying a word. They kept asking me to answer, but I was determined that I was not going to a counselor, so I refused to answer them. (I had the shutting down thing down to a science.) That tactic, however, failed miserably because I still had to go. The counselor knew her job well, because even though I was determined I was not going to speak to her, she was so kind and personable that she had me laughing and smiling in no time. Although I do not remember her name, I still remember her face, and I will always remember her words. I completely opened myself up to her, and I remember her telling me that I was a bright child. Have you ever shut down on God when things seemed to be coming at you at lightning speed and you did not know what to do?

God gently speaks to you, and before you know it you are back in His comfort feeling right at home. It was wonderful that the counselor showed grace that day, and it is even more wonderful that God continues to show grace even when it seems nobody else does.

Now, I know you may wonder about my biological father. Well, I remember craving to know him. There was always speculation of who he was and where he was surfaced from time to time. I wrote letters to him on different occasions, telling him about myself and questioning his whereabouts. There were rumors in my neighborhood that my daddy was playing music at the Neighborhood bar. I was elated, smiling from ear to ear! I was going to meet him.

I could not contain the happiness. There were security guards there, but I mustered up every little bit of energy I had and asked to see the man they called Boss. The guard questioned who I was to him. With my pearly whites I said, "My daddy." My heart thumped and thumped, and my palms grew sweaty as I waited for him to appear. He finally came to the door, and he acted as if he knew me. He picked me up, kissed me on the cheek, and handed me a dollar. I was so excited! He then promised that he would come by to see me after the show, and that I should stay out of the sun because I was getting darker. That dollar meant the world to me; in my eyes I was rich. That was the longest night, because as the clock tick-tock, he never showed. I remember crying myself to sleep, waking periodically to every sound, thinking that maybe he was knocking. I wanted him to know what an angel he had. Perhaps I hoped that one day he would come for me – show interest. If he ever received one of the letters I wrote mattered less now: his heart was not in it.

I would eventually contact him when my oldest child was around the age of two. He had excuse after excuse of why he was not there: "Your mother had someone else", "I was young", blah, blah, blah. I eventually lost contact with him. I used to stare at the picture he sent me. He was a tall lanky, dark, skinny man who probably did not realize the significance that a father plays in the role of his children. But despite it all, God has made me a conqueror.

He has made you one, too.

Prayer

Dear Lord,

Thank you for sheltering and protecting me when I could not protect myself. Thank you for adopting me into your family – a gift of life which you bestowed upon me. I could never repay you. Thank you for loving me this way.

Chapter 2

Imprints

My father did not show up that night that he promised. I was left feeling abandoned. He left a deep hurt within me that I often wished I could forget and put behind me forever, but life does not work quite that way. "The past often steps on the heels of the present." Those painful footsteps from the past made an impression on my young heart that would make it difficult for me to move on and heal until I learned to deal with it. I want to share with you a way to find healing from those deep footprints in your life, as well.

I am writing this in hopes that you will find light at the end of the tunnel, and perhaps you will hold on just a little while longer to God's undying love and mercy. He triumphs! Through Him you can be the shining light that reveals the unwavering love of our *Heavenly* Father.

Amid the chaos of the mess known as "my early life", God created such a beauty. He nurtured love amid loveless-ness. He does that. My purpose in this journey is to bring hope to those who are hurting and to show them that no matter how dreadful the past may have been: God has paved a better future for them that trust Him. I want to open up a world of, "You're not just born to a human: you belong to a Master who lovingly and miraculously created you!

Perhaps the gift that your Creator gave to your parents was misused and abused, or maybe you have been disappointed by the thing's life has thrown at you. No matter the situation you have found yourself in – God can make all things new. Trust me, my friend: God restores. Not only does He restore – he is a way-maker. No circumstance can alter or prohibit your happiness, prosperity, or ability to love and be loved. There is healing that can transcend all obstacles known to man. You must be willing - to go the extra mile to the finish. He is forever by your side.

As we unpack your baggage, my prayer is that you find your inner peace, healing and reasons to love and be loved. So, get comfy, and let us talk about the acknowledgement, the healing factor, letting go, and loving.

ACKNOWLEDGE YOUR PAST, BUT DON'T CAMP THERE

The Chains That Love Broke

Your history is a big part of your life, but it should never be the end all. Your future is by far the greatest thing you can reach for, and it is so much more rewarding than your past. Your past merely provides a backdrop to show why you do some of the things that you do, as well as to pinpoint the deeply hurt areas that could use a little TLC. Your past may have happened, but you can still become a whole, healed individual. You do not in any way, shape or form, must live your life in the shadow of what was.

There comes a point when you must acknowledge what happened, heal, and then move on. There is no point in rehashing what happened or why it happened: it cannot be changed. But it *is* crucial to acknowledge those hurt areas so that they may be properly dealt with and not repeated in your future. People will and do mess up. Let us face it: everybody has faults. The very people who are a part of your life: family, friends, co-workers, et cetera, may have done things that has caused you pain. Even though I did not grow up ideal, I did not expect perfection from my mother. You never truly know the inner struggle of those around you. Maybe they were suffering from some hidden pain of their own. A hurting person tends to hurt other people - but it does not have to continue that way. One of the things that I found extremely therapeutic was keeping a journal of my thoughts and feelings. I never understood how much of a coping mechanism it was for me in my childhood. It was an avenue where I could vent - even if I could not talk to anyone else about what was happening in my life.

Looking back at my early journal entries allowed me to see where I had been hurt and it helped me understand the areas in which I needed help.

Many people have asked me how I was able to walk away from my home at the age of thirteen. Even at a very young age I knew that the environment which I was subjected to was not healthy, and that if I did not find an escape I would be swallowed up in the defeat and despair in which I dwelled. It was not an easy decision in any sense of the word, but it had to be done. I did so with the understanding that my family would demand to know why, and it would perhaps even place upon them guilt for turning a blind eye. I had to live with that fact; however, as a young Christian I knew that God would deliver me, even though I still needed to go through the healing process.

WHAT DO YOU NEED TO ACKNOWLEDGE?

People react and cope differently. Some people become extremely angry at the world while others retreat into themselves. I was incredibly quiet and withdrawn. I was such an inward person that that I was labeled a slow learner and unsociable. I recall totally shutting down at times in the foster home in which I lived, refusing to speak to anyone. times I There are times I cried uncontrollably. My foster mother endured it, though she did not quite understand what was happening with me. As far as she was concerned, I was in a nice home, I had a room of my own and there were nice clothes to boot: therefore, I should have been elated. Do not get me wrong: I appreciated and adored her, but things that had been shoved deep into the core of me had to be dealt with no matter what looked good on the surface. I had to begin to acknowledge the pain.

Acknowledgment must come before the healing stage can happen. Without acknowledgement you live with the idea that hurt did not happen. If you can face it, then you can begin to deal with it. It has always been said that a drunk cannot fix being a drunk if he does not know he is a drunk. What is it that *you* need to acknowledge? What have you pushed into the deep recesses of your heart that keeps you from living abundantly? I do not know what you need to bring forward. Not everyone has had a bad childhood - but everyone has a past of some sort. Are you ready to acknowledge yours so you can move on to your healing? The acknowledgement phase is, first, admitting that there are uncomfortable memories of the past and then asking, "What am I going to do about them?"

One scripture that reinforces the need for us to work from the inside out is, *"First clean the inside of the cup, so that the outside of it may also become clean." Matthew 23:26.* **These** sums up the order: healing happens first on the inside, and then it reflects on the outside. I believe that whatever has happened to you can be healed. God's strength and grace have kept you through the toughest times of your life, and they will be there for you in the future, as well. I assure you that your past story is not your future story. Let God's love continue to keep you. I assure you that He will not let you give up.

DON'T ALLOW THE ENEMY TO CHEW YOU UP

Such a story as the one I have told often sounds the alarm that perhaps we are defeated and that we cannot overcome the circumstances that keep our souls entangled in the lies of the enemy. Defeat is a deceptive thing. Defeat says, "I cannot rise above the circumstances of life." It takes away your will and your sense of control. Defeat takes your purpose in life and chews it up; spitting it out only after it has sucked the spirit of truth and harmony out of it.

As I write this, some of you are still in the process of being chewed up. Have you ever had a perfectly seasoned piece of meat that you just could not wait to devour? You put it in your mouth, and you chewed and chewed, eventually your jaws grew tired. The succulent juice that it once held eventually dissipated and you no longer got any joy out of it, but you kept on chewing. After all, you wanted to grind it so that you could swallow it easily. However, there are some pieces of meat that are just too tough to swallow, and once you have chewed the flavor out of them, you just spit them out. It is no longer pleasing to your taste buds.

Releasing yourself from the grinding jaws of past failure involves believing in *whose you are*, not in *where you have been*. Allowing the Enemy to chew you up and spit you out is keeps you stuck in a moment, a circumstance or a situation that is *not* a true reflection of you or the God you serve. God gave you power and authority over what you allow to control your spirit, and we must be willing to evict whatever is not of God. Make it flee! It has no right or room in your life. Fight for your victory. The person God made you to be and the person you are can never lose their flavor. You are not disposable, and the enemy has no dominion over you. In fact, *you* have the dominion, and you can knock out any teeth that the devil has in his mouth and set yourself free! We must learn to take back with authority those promises God has spoken over us. I am not saying that the power to win is easy. The power to win is that you are made strong by God's strength, and strength in God never becomes weak. Go ahead and flex your blessed muscles and declare your victory. Psalm 62:7 says, *"My salvation and glory depend on God, my Strong Rock."* If He Who is your Rock says that your strength lies in Him, then how could your power to persevere possibly be dependent on your past circumstances? Acknowledge them, but then take control over them. *Then* you will be on your way to healing!

13

<u>Prayer</u>

"Lord you have given me the victory. Remind me to always walk uprightly. In my weakness, you are strong. Again, my strength is always renewed in you."

Chapter Three

Roots

I grew up in the church. On Sunday mornings adorned in a dress, stockings and black patent leather shoes. It did not matter if the stockings had holes throughout: we were not allowed any excuse or escape from entering the Lord's house. If we were not sick, we got up and went to church. My dear Aunt would be dressed to the tee. She had plenty of big hats and dresses to last for a multitude of Sundays. Church, like getting an education, was required of us. My grandmother and Aunt, devout Christians, would have it no other way. We did not ask questions. We knew the rule: "As for me and my house, we will serve the Lord."

Mount Zion Baptist Church a small town in Ohio - is where I got my footing. I remember all the old hymns: "By and By" as well as "Going up yonder". I used to watch my grandmother and aunt sing so loudly and joyfully. Perhaps I did not quite understand the joy, but I am sure perhaps, like me, they had more than enough reasons to praise the Almighty. Eventually, a church bus came around picking up the children up for a church that was on the other side of town. I recall many of us getting on the bus. I felt comfortable – for many of the kids - it was an opportunity to cut loose. I think the church bit off a little bit more than they could chew when they sent that bus after us, but they still came to pick me up by car long after the bus rides ceased. I enjoyed it, and I made lots of friends. It was an escape from the life I knew.

I joined the youth group, and most of my weekends were spent with one of the many families I became close with. They saw a hurting child, and they took me in, nurtured me, and turned this once shy, withdrawn child into a lively one.

I spent many summers at the Church of God Youth Camps. It was there that I gave my life to God. It was a momentous occasion: I felt the Spirit of God fill me, and I wept and prayed. I told God about everything, and I felt such calmness. I suddenly had a reason to keep fighting. I began to see my way out of the defeat, and I knew then that no matter what, God would hold my hand. Even at that young age I heard the voice of God through the midst of the trials that surrounded me. Some will say, "How did you hear Him?" I heard Him when I cried, wanted to quit, and did not see a reason to go on. He held me in those moments, and I knew that somehow this was not the end. It was just a fraction of my life, and if I persevered, I would find the strength to rise above my circumstances and perhaps help someone else up. It was that private conversation that never left my spirit and continually reminded me that He was there. Often what we need to be reminded of is that someone cares. It is our responsibility to be a light to those who are in their darkest moments – who see's little hope around, yet enough reasons to quit. There is nothing in the whole world that happens that God does not know about. The beauty of His grace and mercy is that He knows how many times you have cried. He knows everywhere you hurt. He wants to help you: will you allow Him to?

Often when a person has suffered great emotional, physical or mental distress, they run to others to fill the void in hopes that the sore place in which they find themselves will somehow miraculously disappear. All it does is apply a bandage to mask the hurt. When the temporary bandage comes off the pain resurfaces. We often resume looking for other means to fill the void. It can come in the form of alcohol, sex, searching for acceptance… You are aware of the list. Brokenness can manifest in many forms.

SIFTING THROUGH YOUR PAST

Your roots of the where, why and how do count, but the most important root you have is whose you are, - your connection to our Creator, the One who has the first and last say. He is the One who can take crumpled paper and smooth it out again.

Psalm 46:1 says, "God is our refuge and strength, a helper who is always found in times of trouble."

17

Free Indeed

As you read this, I pray that God will send you a breath of assurance and renewed love from the only True One who can sustain you. The first and most important factor in confronting the skeletons in your closet is opening that door: open it with all the strength you have. Pull every one of them out, and start putting them in the garbage where they belong. If you must cry while you do it, that is ok. If you must scream at the top of your lungs, release it... I must be honest with you; this is my most difficult task. Why take note of the things that hurt so badly? I had gotten so use to existing with the pain, never acknowledging that I had been wounded – always wearing a cupcake smile. I mean, I stayed sweet even when my heart was thinly held together with tape that had to be replaced on occasion. I could not trust - would not trust. It just meant too much vulnerability. Love has a way exposing our deepest insecurities. Love seeks out the wounds – exposing them – causing the darkness to be shattered by the light. When light enters darkness is forced to leave. God is the greatest love you can experience with the brightest light you could ever imagine.

What happens to a captured bird when it is released? It finds the wings that God created it to have, and it learns to fly. You also were destined to fly. Every creature has a purpose. Man's purpose is to walk in the authority of Love. You are not who "they" say you are. You are a King's kid, and you just might have to remind some folks of that! The Good Book tells you that you are a chosen generation, a royal priesthood and a holy nation. You are destined for greatness because The Great I AM dwells within you.

It will take some true self-introspection to figure out what needs to be let go. Identifying your areas of improvement not only improves your outlook, but it also brings to the forefront your faulty thinking that plays a very real role in how you view yourself and your circumstances.

The mind is the most powerful tool that has kept many a purposed folk bound to what *was* instead of reaching for what could be. I was such a person for an exceptionally long time. I lived in the sea of regret, condemnation and shame. Understand this, My Friend: today is the day you need to decide that your past will no longer hinder, manipulate and plunge you into the depths of despair by believing the lie that the Enemy uses to cripple you and leave you stagnated and blind.

Many people feel that if they are functioning in their environment, they really could not ask for more. Well, I am here to shut down the myth of just functioning. You, man and woman of God, were not created to just function. God did not give his only begotten Son so that you may just exist. No: the purpose of the cross was that all the burdens of the world would remain there, and that life would resurrect itself. Not only would it resurrect, but it would shine brighter than ever before! Death happened at the cross, but life arose from it.

19

Whatever is holding you back, keeping you from moving forward – let it go. There is not room in your future for lack. John 3:16 says it best, "God so loved the world that He gave His only begotten Son - that whoever shall believe in Him shall not die but have everlasting life." Your past cannot lay claim on what does not belong to it. God's only Son died for your past so that you may live in your future.

OUR COPING TOOLS

It is important to discuss the outlets that we use to cover our pain. Many times, alcohol is used to make hurt places seem better for a while. It is ineffective for the long term because as soon as those moments of mind-altering highs leave, you will come crashing back down You quickly learn that at the first binge you start on a path of many binges until the point where you do not even recognize who you are. You become a prisoner of the alcohol by bowing to the bondage of your past. The blind leads the blind. My mother was drunk most of my young life. I knew that was not who she was, but rather what had her chained. Most people do not say, "Hey I'm going to be an alcoholic today." It happens because people hold onto too much far too long.

What coping methods have you used or seen others use. Some use sex as an outlet to cover up the pain. Seeking pleasure in a touch from the opposite sex. Sex being used as a method of self-indulging feel-good medication. Sex was not meant to be shared with anyone and everyone willing to give it. Just like alcohol, it claims its victim with the temporary sensation of good feelings. You forget the immorality - because you need to be touched physically. Somehow that sensation of touch, even if it is just for a moment, makes you feel loved. It is a false sense of love that deceives so many.

We all have fallen prey to the arrangement of pain and brokenness at some point in our lives. Neither sex nor drugs have the power to fill that emptiness. It is the trickery of the devil that comes to fill your head with those conniving lies. The habits that get abused, lead only to more hurt and pain, thus entangling you so much that they take a long time to undo. When you search to fill that void through sex - you birth responsibilities which you are unprepared for. Then you are left to figure out what love is so that you can love what you have created. Do you see where I am going with this?

We use a lot of coping skills that are dysfunctional and the ones I listed are the short form: I am sure you are aware there are many. The only true way to move past things that have caused us pain is by way of healing and forgiving.

THE SEARCH FOR TRUTH

Truth is not found in the devices which we find ourselves enslaved to - it lies within knowing who we are in God. You do not have to hold on to anything that is not of God. And in the mighty name of God I pray release over your life. You are not that which has tried to hold you hostage. You are blessed. Your God is the ultimate loving God; He will never leave you nor forsake you. He created you, and with that - you can stand up straight and be proud because His mercy has already been given unto you. You do not have to earn it. It is given to you freely and willingly. Can you accept your gift?

It is yours for the taking. You have suffered long enough. Lay down those burdens and take the hand that God has extended to you. I had to learn to love me – my strengths and my weaknesses. I had to give up my will to correct things – and rest in the fullness of God. As I begun to release the chains of bondage - joy began to fill those once empty places. I promise that where there was hurt, you will be filled with joy. Where there was a void, you will be filled with purpose. Your circumstances do not stand a chance when you just give Him praise.

He loves you – every part of you.

YOU NEED THE CHURCH

The church family is an integral part to your relationship with God. I said church family because the church is not the building or a place you go. The church resides in you. Being connected with those with like-minded faith is paramount. When the church joins in unity, within it resides a power to be reckoned with. Your church family should be a place where the hurting can find refuge – not condemnation – but understanding, patience, forgiveness and love. All that God stands for should be reflected in the church body. If you are connected to the right people who have the heart of God – you can find healing under their wings. It is important that during this acknowledgement phase that you seek out the help of the church pastor, a licensed counselor, or anyone who has a significant positive influence on your life - who can encourage you along the way as you discover your blessed self. More importantly you must draw closer to your Heavenly Father.

Study the Word and seek His presence. Take time for prayer, praise and developing that personal relationship with Him. Do not for a moment think that the road to recovery can be done single-handedly. As you fight through your moments of weakness, you will need the encouragement and support of those around you. God can send the right people into your life at the right time to assist with your growth. Do not be intimidated or afraid to open to those extending a helping hand to you. You were not created to go it alone.

There are situations and obstacles you may find yourself in - which you have little or no control. In such circumstances, the power to overcome them lies in what you do with what is happening. Do you allow it to stop you, or does it make you want to try harder? Often where you feel you have no control is where you are the most powerful, because you can choose your actions or your reactions. Your circumstances can either cause you to faint, or they can cause you to grow stronger.

YOUR RESPONSE TO YOUR PAST

It is also imperative to understand any and every part that you played in what has happened or what continues to happen. You must alter some behaviors, attitudes, or thoughts in order to bring about the results that you are searching for. For example, victim mentality breeds hopelessness, and you should avoid it at all cost. You can decide to use those obstacles that you face to propel you to a better place, or you can allow them to defeat you and keep you demoted. I would rather choose to be propelled into a much stronger, wiser me. Find that strength within - it is there: just give it a chance.

I had to decide if I was going live and make decisions based on hurt, or was I going to discover the healing that God already said was mine and move forward. When you delve into your personhood, the mighty strength of God who lives within you comes, full front. It is so amazing to know that God, who is so merciful and so loving, who knows your name, wants nothing more than to give you His best. Within His perfection He restores the peace and the joy. Sometimes you must be broken so that God can build you the way He needs and expects you to be. It is not until you are fully broken that you are able to see the God in you shine ever so brightly.

YOU ARE LOVED!

God does love you. One of the biggest misconceptions is that when we go through difficult times, somehow, we are lacking something, or we are not well-liked or loved – even thinking that God has forgotten us. Studying the word of God will breathe life into you and renew your hope. It will take you from your dark places and reassure you by the power of His grace, mercy and love. There is nothing on this green earth that can separate you from the One who created you. Grasping such a truth changes everything: it adds perspective amid the confusion.

I gave my life over to the Lord at a young age, but I cannot say that my relationship with Him was where it should have been. Yes, I knew Him – even turned my life over to Him. Let us face it, we have all played church at one time or another – going through the motions – but once we stepped outside of that church building, we would return to doing everything the world's way. The truth of the matter is I think it took some of that – ok, maybe a *lot* of that -- to finally understand that I needed to either join the winning team whole-heartedly or continue to live life with a broken wing. Maybe that old saying really does have a bit of truth to it: "A hard head makes a soft…" (I know you can finish that.) Sometimes I wondered how many times that I would allow myself to keep hitting that brick wall – the obvious wall that was not moving no matter how hard I hit it my way. Surrendering had not made it into my vocabulary. If I had allowed myself to connect with the right family, I could have alleviated some of those pitfalls. What I want you to know – what I *need* you to know - is that you must fellowship with people who are also born again. The worst thing that you can begin to believe is that repentance mean you can weather it all alone. Fellowship facilitates the growth of your relationship with God. Surround yourself with mentors. Be around those who can effectively model what a life with Christ looks like. I am one of those who tried to do it on my own. When I went on to College, the support system that I once had was suddenly gone. Even though my belief in and love for God had not changed, I was no longer being spiritually fed or surrounded by those who could help guide me. Ultimately, I was little-by-little being guided by the world. I began to own what I knew was not God's way. I had never cussed in my life – but once I entered college, I did what everyone else was doing. I did not even sound right saying it – imagine that. I had a boyfriend for the first time who would also introduce me to alcohol. I knew it was wrong – I wanted to fit in. I wanted to belong.

I spent most of my life feeling like I was the strange apple and everybody else was the cool orange. I wanted them to like me. I wanted to be them. If I could act like the orange, then maybe I would blend in so much that my differences would not be noticed.

I stopped going to church because it just was not cool. I ran from the One who created me to be who I am – who thought I was worth the touch of uniqueness. God wants to draw us closer to Him so that we are protected, but often we run away from that protection seeking out fulfillment through other means. The reality is that any fulfillment sought outside of the realm of God is short-lived. Leaving the comfort of your God to find comfort in the world only leads to a dead-end road.

THE VALUE OF TRIALS

The funny thing about life's lessons is that we will all make mistakes, and we will always learn. That is life. You cannot escape it, nor should you want to. Every lesson that you have learned has, in some way, shaped who you are. The lessons that you learn when you are out on the battlefield should do one thing: they should make you stronger. I can honestly say that I am much stronger now than I ever was. I am stronger, not only because I have weathered some storms, but because I have weathered them still standing. I am standing, not in my own might, but I am standing because God held me up, and comforted me when I had no one to comfort me. He was my Shield when I did not have the will or desire to protect myself.

What you must digest is that *you* may leave the presence of God, but He never, ever leaves nor forsakes you. God stays with you no matter how far you stray, taps you on our shoulder and says, "I'm right here, come home when you are ready." God does not force Himself on you. He waits and lets you do what you are going to do. Either you will fall, and He will catch you, or you will return before you fall. His door is open.

Have you ever knocked on a door and banged till the whole neighborhood heard you? No matter how hard you knocked, those in the house either did not hear you, or they did not want to be bothered. God's love is so deep and magnificent that He opens the door even before you have a chance to knock. He knows where you are at any given moment, and He knows when you have reached the end of your rope. Surely, you are saying, "Why would He allow you to come back to Him when you willfully left His presence?" His love for you is unconditional, and He will forever love you. Write this on your heart: there is nothing that you can ever do to make Him not love you. Nothing! You are his child, and He loves you. He loves you just the way you are. There may be things that He knows you need to change, but what better way to see you through them than to love you through them?

Oh, if you could just step away from what the world tells you! Maybe you are believing that you are nobody, unlovable, lonely, unwanted, etc. If you are harboring anything but love for yourself, I say stop right now in the name of Jesus. What a beautiful creation you are – perfect in his sight. He created you in His image. Listen, My Friend, God does not make any mistakes –

not even with you. You are loved as if you were His only child – cherished and adored.

You are creative, purposed, and irreplaceable. If you must speak it when you wake in the morning, in the noonday, evening or night, speak your truth. Change can only happen when you understand that if you're telling yourself anything other than what God says you are - then you truly need to rewrite the script, because God says He created you just the way He wanted you. If nobody else in the world can see from which cloth you are made, then that is their problem and not yours. It is not your responsibility to adopt any ideology of what they say, because they did not create you, or anyone else. Your parents did not even create you: they carried you as a vessel. But God placed you there, and He knew your name before you were even conceived. When you bask in that truth, My Friend, you will begin to see yourself as God sees you.

Prayer: *Lord I need you now and always. The truth of who I am resides not in who others say I am – but in whom you say that I am. I am your child. Lack does not exist in the realm of your holiness. I have everything I need, as you promised to supply all my needs. I know sometimes I fail to ask for the desires of my heart - yet I know you understand. I know you have already provided access to everything that is for my good. Allow me to go boldly and confidently into the world telling of your goodness. I am a child of*

Free Indeed

the Light - born again by the Spirit of God. Teach me to speak your truth always so that I walk with my head held up and not down. Yes, Lord, I know you favored me. What the enemy meant for my bad - You turned around for my good!

Chapter 4

Control Your Thoughts

Often our learned behaviors become the same ones we act upon. This is true of thoughts as well. The more we stare at our circumstances - instead of focusing on God - reinforces the wrong actions, thoughts and beliefs. We see it (physical), we believe it (heart) and we act it. This is so automatic that we do not even realize we are doing it. We end up speaking those things in our life that we either grew up hearing or got used to seeing. Our thoughts become our words, which are then received and absorbed into our heart.

Of course, nobody wakes up in the morning and says things like, "I'm going to tell myself all the wrong things that I have done," or, There had to be something wrong with me or it wouldn't have happened," or, "Well, if it had not been for the way I was raised…" or, "So-and-so-hurt me, so I'm going to make sure nobody ever gets a chance to hurt me again: I'm going to hurt them before   they   hurt   me

."

The victim mentality only keeps you bound to what was, and you cannot get free from it unless you are willing to confront the negative talk that you are speaking to yourself. The funny thing is that the people who are doing this hardly recognize it themselves: it takes someone else to point it out to them. That is when it becomes obvious that we have already bought into the many lies and misconceptions that others have fed us. The feeder is no longer needed because the one being fed has become his or her own feeder! It takes someone to lovingly point out such behavior and show you that what you are thinking or believing is not your truth.

It is not easy to fight this enemy of self; we are often our own worst enemy. The easiest lie that can be bought into is the one that you have told yourself. Yes, you, My Friend. Some people will tell you anything - it is up to you to hold on to your truth – the truth of what God says about you.

The mind is a powerful thing. It holds so much information that sometimes it wants to replay events like a tape recorder. Not only does it replay them, but it begins to tell you little tales as well:

"You can't make it," or,

"You've failed again. Just give up," or,

"You can't trust anyone!"

The devil's quickest way to conquer you is by way of your mind.

If he can infiltrate your mind, before long he is in your heart, and soon you begin to act on his lies. You must protect the gateway of the mind and deny the devil access to it. Your current circumstances do not mean that you are a failure or that you will not see brighter days. They do not mean that because so-and-so hurt you that everyone else will repeat the action. Those are lies of the enemy, and you must recognize them as such if you are going to experience healing.

HEALING

Healing emotionally, physically, and mentally from the past is a particularly important factor in releasing a brighter future for you. Without healing, you are bound to continue on with a life of pain: if you are not releasing that baggage that has you so bound up, you will take it into your future.

Removing yourself from situations which are not conducive to your overall health is the right place to start, but it is not the end. Sweeping it under the rug is what we most often do with painful experiences and situations. That is not a proper cleaning. Neither is tying up your trash as tightly as you possibly can in hopes that the smell will not escape and infiltrate your home. If the trash is not properly disposed of, no matter how tightly the bag is sealed, it will eventually permeate your home. You cannot clean your house that way, and I am sure emotional recovery from your past would be ineffective that way as well.

Look at it this way: if you do not dispose of what has held you down, then more than likely you will carry that same stench into your relationships and future situations. Release the garbage. Refuse to weigh yourself down with the baggage of yesterday.

Letting Go

Sometimes you must let go,

Even when what you are holding on to is all you know.

The cost of holding on outweighs,

the cost of letting go.

The baggage – the stagnation – is too heavy to carry You are longing to be free.

Open your hands, what holds on to you, will just let you be.

So much to gain and nothing to lose

Letting go, what will you choose?

Joy, peace, and life begin at the start,

But we must live to do our part.

Do not carve what was in the sand,

But write the victory; that is the heavenly plan!

Too blessed to be pressed

About what is already gone.

The future is bright make peace with the past, then you will walk into victory at last. Deuteronomy 32:39 God makes known the fact that He is the only God that has the power to bring healing to His people. He rescues you from what is choking you, breathes life back into you. That is powerful, because often we allow people, things and circumstances that have absolutely no power over us at all to have power over our lives. So, we give our past, hurts, disappointments and thoughts the power to manipulate us into thinking that we are nothing but victims of circumstances. What a lie! If you have not heard it anywhere else, the Bible clearly says that God is all-powerful. That means that victory and healing are already yours. One of the most amazing stories in the Bible that gives us a glimpse of a most painful past is Hosea's marriage to his prostitute wife, Gomer. Let us look at this scenario. Could you imagine a man who wants to find the rib of his rib waking up one faithful morning and saying, "Yes! This is the day I'm to put a ring on a prostitute!" You are thinking, "Ludicrous," right? That would be laughable to most people, but God ordered Hosea to take the prostitute Gomer as a wife and bare children with her. Now, Hosea probably scratched his head like, "Now, Father, let me make sure that I am hearing you right. You want me, Hosea, to go marry Gomer and make babies with her?" To make a long story short, yes: that is what God wanted him to do. God had a special purpose for what He asked Hosea to do. He wanted to make an example out of them to demonstrate the relationship between Himself and the nation of Israel. You see, Gomer was out in the world doing her own thing – selling her body – probably to make a living. I'm sure she was thinking, "Yes! A good man has come to marry me!" That was like jackpot to her. Now, at first in this story, things were blissful. Gomer probably thought, "I have begun a new life." I am sure she never truly dealt with her past, which, being left unchecked, began to creep back into her life once her new life began to wear off. Maybe she began to think that raising the kids was more work than she had bargained for, so she resorted to her old lifestyle.

Hosea, I am sure, was disappointed, but through it all he brought her back from her depths of despair and welcomed her back home with full forgiveness. I am sure that many other things took place once she returned. Hosea, being a man of God, was a man of prayer.

He took the problems straight to the only One who could heal them.

In the same way, Israel would one day return to acknowledge that God was God.

No situation is so messed up or helpless that God cannot bring restoration to it. Just like Hosea and Gomer, we must remember that God is not keeping record or score of our wrongs. He says, "I am that 'I AM'". Are you ready to let him heal all your dark places? Isn't it time for light to come shining through? Isn't it time that you replace the bad with all the good that is available to you? My Friend, your fulfilled life awaits you. Walk into your healing. Today is a better time to start than ever. Perhaps you are not selling your body, but maybe you are damaging yourself through holding on to things you need to let go of. We must stop prostituting ourselves to our failures and misfortunes. We must protect ourselves through the covering of our almighty God, who holds the capability to bring wholeness and healing, so that we may return to our Hosea brand new. My Friend, once you step away from what is *not* for you, you will walk into what *is*. This is a magnificent display of beauty for ashes!

Chapter Five

Love

Love is such a complex word, and few of us have experienced it in its entirety or have an accurate understanding of what it really is. This concept is worth visiting because it, too, will affect how you treat people and how you allow yourself to be treated. I want to reveal to you what God views as love. Corinthians 13:4-8 describes love as being patient and kind; not envious or boastful; it is not irritable or resentful; nor rejoicing in wrongdoing but rejoicing in truth. Love bears all things, believes hopes, endures, and never ends. This scripture is so powerful: it tells us that love never ends. Love cannot end because it is what is on the inside that reflects on the outside. Love is given by God, so nobody and nothing has the power to steal what is on the inside of you. Perhaps those who have trouble receiving love does so because they have yet to learn to love themselves first. We must accept the love that God has shown us before we can show it to others. If your love bank is empty, I encourage you to fill up on

God. He gave you all the love you need when He sent you Jesus. Once you get what He is giving, then it fills you so full that that resentfulness, irritation, and all other spiritual "drains" have no space to reside.

THE DIFFICULTY WITH LEARNING TO LOVE

It is easy to become confused about love. You may not have seen it modeled within the early stages of life through your parents or extended family, and so it gets distorted in all sorts of ways. It is now a subject of great controversy in the American community because of some of the hardships we face as people. You can see a broken system with the inability to love and receive love through the outrageous number of single parent-homes that exist today. There are an astronomical number of women choosing to go it alone because of the likelihood of a failed relationship. Instead of people learning to deal with issues within the relationship - many people are just deciding to go it alone. It comes down to issues such as un-forgiveness, self-esteem, misunderstanding of love, grudges and looking at life from the back door. Let us discuss one of those situations: the absentee father and what implications it has upon on the children. Being raised without a father or a father figure gives me insight about that. It was not necessarily that my father was not there, but the truth of the matter is that there was nobody else that filled his shoes. No grandparents, uncles or mentors were around to teach and be an example of what a man should do. I rarely saw a couple living as husband and wife, or even raising kids together. Families often consisted of grandmothers raising their daughters' children, or a mother raising children alone. That is what I grew up with, so the healthy "together" situation just did not exist.

As I moved out of my foster mother's home, I was placed out in the world to survive without support. I married a man who really did not take the time to know who I was, nor did I know who he was. We did the marriage dance, the vows, the clothing and the party, but after all that was said and done, it was all we had. We were not in the least bit prepared for marriage. It is never enough to say "I do" in front of God and the church. A true relationship is so much more than what can be seen with the natural eyes, and vows alone are not enough to sustain it. We were two totally different beings with uncompromising ideas of what should or should not happen in a relationship. My idea of love was that we were committed to one another, and if we would just talk everything over, then we would make it through anything that might arise. As far as I knew, we were both Christians, but that is hardly enough to have a successful relationship. There were so many missing pieces of the puzzle that should be formed in any relationship. Where was the discussion about finances, children, problem management, compromising, etc.? I really did not know what was required of a wife because I did not grow up around women who were married. That caused a problem, because I went into the relationship believing that because I married him, I had to take whatever he did to me. That is what I learned from my family, and I was never taught any different.

A relationship built on love requires an understanding of compromising – not always trying to be right – and learning to agree to disagree. In addition to all those things there must be respect and the agreement that you both deserve the best from one another. In a love commitment you should inspire, motivate, encourage, and challenge each other. God should always be the center cord of the relationship. When issues arise, then both, not just one, must be willing to sacrifice.

Know who you are and what you want before jumping into a relationship with anyone. Make sure that you are a whole individual coming in and your self-esteem is where it should be. Make sure that you are not changed for the worse going into a relationship. Your potential mate should forever bring out the best in you. The two of you should be better together than apart. If you did not know how to swim, would you jump into too-deep waters without a lifejacket? I would hope not. You know the result could be that you would either drown or come up choking. The same is true with a relationship. Surround yourself with people who have been married successfully, and do not have too much pride to ask them what works for them. Having a pastor or licensed professional talk you through the tough topics that you probably have washed over are a good start. There is nothing worse than jumping into a relationship headfirst without first discussing the things that a relationship consists of.

Self-esteem is a biggie. I have seen others (and I have done it myself as well) jump into a relationship just for the comfort of it. It did not matter if we liked any of the same things or even if we were headed in the same direction. What is wrong with being held? I was giving and giving and always felt poured out and empty. It was a time waster and a hindrance to my purpose and destiny of finding the one who was intended for me.

HOW GOD OPENS YOUR EYES

God places people in your life for a reason. Often, we do not know why or even care to speculate about the reason. Over the last two years the most amazing thing has happened to me: people have come into my life that has enriched my growth as a person. I am forever grateful to the flood of motivation, encouragement, determination and challenges that God has sent my way. It has changed my life for the better. Worth mentioning in greater detail is a wonderful man that has shown me the person I am, and not the person I thought I was.

We come across many friends throughout our lifetimes, but great is the friend who becomes your biggest cheerleader, confidant and motivator. Mine has been a blessing beyond compare in my life. He reminded me that I am not to be controlled by the past, or the things that it consists of. He helped me realize that I am a talented, extremely creative individual who was gifted and purposed. In addition to the good things that he helped reveal, he also helped me see those skeletons that I myself did not realize where still in my life. He helped me to achieve a higher level of thinking that I had run away from for such a long time. He showed up at just the right season of my life, as God intended. People will come and go in your lifetime, and each one has a different purpose. Some come as a blessing, others come to teach a lesson, and some come to test you. The childhood motivators were there as a blessing to get me through my childhood, but when you are no longer a child - it is destiny time. Destiny time is when you are taught to come into your complete self. You embrace the fullness of who you are and accept it all completely. Finally, the trials that come were never meant to kill you: they were sent to strengthen you and move you into more meaningful moments and times in your life. Isn't it wonderful when someone is able to see the God in you, and you celebrate together that part of you? It is amazing! True friends come as a breath of fresh air. You can be yourself – your totally nerdy, quirky, artsy, self – and a true friend will love you just as you are. I love to look at it as "laying down the pretense". One of the greatest things I learned about myself when he crossed my path was this: I still was carrying some hurt. That was the most difficult thing to realize. All those years I felt like I had truly let it all go I had hidden it deeper. I was comfortable existing. I struggled with that truth – it was staring me right in the face. I did not want to shove it deeper any longer. I wanted to expose it completely - I just could not afford to continue to live beneath God's best. It was my wake-up call. Was that His purpose in my life? If it were- it worked. I had hit that fork in the road that was waiting for the right move. I did not want to live that life anymore. I began to see my value (though it was not the person I let out much), even though it felt like the wind had been knocked of me. What was being knocked out just did not belong. It reminds me that God is the potter and we are the clay. Trust the process – you are being remolded into masterpieces. Growing hurts, but it is worth it.

Have you ever tried to be someone you are not? The funny thing is when I was out in the world, I used to go barhopping with my friends, and to fit in I used to drink what they were drinking, even though deep inside I did not want it. I would get wasted – truly wasted – off one Long Island iced tea. One! Then the tears would come like a waterfall. (Yes, I was the crying drinker.) People often say when you are drunk you do not fully grasp what you are doing. I have to say that is not all true. When I would get drunk – all the hurts and pains would surface – I knew that the life I was living was the farthest from what God intended. I hid in that shame but covered it up with a smile. Now, I knew better, but it was what everyone else was doing. I did not want to be a fun buster, or a sore loser. I eventually stopped going to the bars with my friends because I began to realize that a true friend takes you as you are, even if you are not doing the same things that they are doing.

RUNNING

When life hands us a raw deal, the thing we do most often is run away from the loving arms of the Heavenly Father. Instead of looking to Him who is our Rock and Shield, we lock Him out. Perhaps we lock Him out because somehow, we feel let down or disappointed. We become so upset with Him – because He has all control – that we begin to question why He allows things to happen to us.

God never promised that life would be easy, or that you would never have to be tested. The trials are what shape you up – build up your endurance. Imagine wanting to lose weight, but you do not want the work that it would require of you. Yes, exercising can be daunting and tiring, but the results are what you are after. The process to get the results will require some pain, sweat and exhaustion. Exhaustion does not kill you: it builds the tenacity that you will need to carry you further. Don't faint or run away from your mountain moments: once you get to the top of the place you deemed too far to reach, you will understand the purpose in the pain and in that still voice in you that keeps saying, "Push." If you ever need strong arms around you that will not let you go, look no further: Jesus is right there. My Friend, the only things you should be running from are the lies you tell yourself, the thoughts and the behaviors that do not reflect your best self and the people who mean you no good. These are reasons, without a doubt, to run. In fact, run, Baby, run, but let God join you in the sprint. It is important, then, to discern the things from which you need to run and that which causes you to stand. Your journey depends on your strength and faith in God.

TRUST

Trust or rather, the lack of thereof, has caused havoc within our own lives and in the lives of those closest to us. When life happens, we avoid trusting others as a means of protecting ourselves from experiencing hurt again. We guard ourselves from the intended harm, either real or imagined. I had learned to distrust people because the people who were responsible for me failed to do the basics. When a child's most basic needs – food, clothing, attention, love, and protection, to name a few – are not being met, it breeds within the child a distrust for her environment. I was a quiet child. There were many attempts to molest me by individuals who were close to me. People who should have never even thought such things. Perhaps the fact that I was so quiet meant that I would be less probable that I would speak up. To an extent, it was true. I never wanted to hurt anyone. I could not imagine hurting my loved ones by confessing to them that a relative had crossed boundaries.

In my mind I felt like I could just avoid that person. I became extremely good at avoiding the situation whenever possible. That person being an authority figure in my life - just imagine how difficult that was. When such things like this happen a healthy view of people and their behaviors becomes disjointed. I hid a lot in my heart, because I internalized it: "Well, if I wasn't well built…", or, "Maybe if my butt didn't stick out, then maybe he wouldn't look at me…." It was all "If only I..." *I* held the blame. I became very insecure around people. If a child cannot trust the environment in which he or she resides, then mistrusting people is going to be one of the symptoms. It took me many, many years to understand that it was not about me, but him. I did not do anything to cause him to touch me. The lie we often tell ourselves is that something happened because we somehow were not good enough. I wrongfully condemned myself.

Wouldn't it be nice to be able to quickly recognize that faulty thinking from the start? It is not that the abused one has a problem, but rather that the abusers inflict hurt on another because *they* have a problem. How much clarity would it bring if only we could understand this? How much quicker could healing begin? Going through life suspicious of everyone is a most dreadful way to live.

Everybody becomes suspect when you cannot trust. You believe they have faltered even if they have not wronged you. You hear things that they did not even say. Have you ever tried to decipher the meaning of a person's word? "Well they said _____, but I know they meant _____..." You become the best judge of character one has ever to meet... or not! What they did becomes (in your mind) what *everyone* did or is going to do. It is a "failure meets failure" life. This type of life is so beneath God's absolute best intentions for you! When pain causes you to distrust the world, God will show you that He can be trusted. When you trust God then His eyes become your eyes, and you never have to question who is friend or foe. Trusting God as your Source and resource removes the doubt that you have about yourself and about others.

Chapter Six

Know Better

There are things that happened in your life, My Friend, that you had no control over. Stop blaming yourself for other people's craziness. You did not deserve it. You did not cause it. The truth of the matter is rather we blame ourselves or others; placing blame does not solve the problem. It does not change what has happened. Blame just gives us the excuse to stay in pain. It gives us the excuse to keep partying in our pity. What if they did hurt you? What if you hurt you? Even with that you can heal – you can move on and grow. We often miss the miracle of life. If we are still living and breathing, we have a new opportunity to turn things around for ourselves. The biggest control we do have

over life is how we react to it. Your reaction could either help you or hinder you.

The miracle, My Friend, is that you are here. Yes, you may have experienced some mishaps, bumps, headaches, and gut punches, but you are here. God never intended for those who did not take care of His gift to prevent you from coming into your own. The love and mercy of God endures. It endures through your pain and growth stages. You are pregnant with purpose, My Friend, and you can operate in the fullness of the God - who resides within you. You will not faint, nor will you fail.

God does not make damaged goods, My Friend, so even though you have been hurt, every smudge that was applied to you was immediately washed away by the blood of Jesus. He makes everything that has been smudged like new again. You are going to lay down that burden of what they did and how they did it. Kings' kids stand tall with shoulders squared. The enemy cannot touch you now. When you get to where you rebuke the things that have jumped on your back, seeking to destroy the spirit within you.

When you begin to walk in your victory – you show others how to walk in theirs. The enemy wants to see you down in despair, but God gave you power to carry through. Don't you know that what was meant to kill you did not? Who is that with a smile as bright as the sun, with eyes shining with a great spirit? You are a ray of light from God. The enemy cannot have your best unless you willingly give it away. The devil is defeated and always has been. *He* has no future. He is after *your* future. He is after *your* happiness, *your* joy, peace and love. Tell it to flee and I promise you it will. There is power in that Word - speak it.

You are the victor, not the victim. Now you know better! God's better!

FORGIVENESS

We tend to internalize things that have happened to us, often placing blame where it does not belong. Some of the things that have happened are partially due to our responsibility or irresponsibility, not so much a direct cause of what happened. (We will touch on responsibility a little later.) Forgiveness is a must: you cannot heal without forgiveness. Who should the forgiveness begin with? If you said yourself, then, my Friend, you have some understanding of healing. The one who plays the most important role in forgiveness is you. *Ephesians 4:32 says, "Be kind and compassionate to one another, forgiving one another, just as God also forgave you in Christ."*

You can stop punishing yourself for the past. The inability to forgive keeps you holding on and causes you to stagnate. God forgives you, and He forgives the offenders, so why don't you forgive yourself? You deserve to move on, but you cannot move on if you do not allow yourself to move on. I said you are the most important person in the forgiveness picture because at the end of the day, you are the only person who stands in the way of who you *weren't* meant to be and who you *are* supposed to be. People can do a lot of damage to you, but you must make the decision that you will not pick up any more baggage - leave it where the offenders dropped it.

We must stop thinking that we must carry every load that is offered to us. Being able to forgive yourself - prepares you to be able to forgive those who have hurt you. If you hold on to what happened, it begins to eat away at your inner being. It fills you with resentment, despair, loss of control, hatred, and the list goes on... It does not eat away at the other person; they probably have not the slightest idea of the torment in which you are taking yourself through.

Imagine a divorced couple. One has already moved on and is, perhaps, seeing someone else, while the other party is entangled in a web of How, when and why of the situation. They find themselves standing in place, unable to move forward because the life they knew has them so tangled up that they cannot find an exit. It consumes their entire being. Divorce is an ugly thing in every sense of the word, and when it hits the fan, what do you do? What happens when you have tried everything imaginable, and now it is over? Do you keep looking at the photo albums of what you had, or do you face the future with optimistic hope for what lies ahead? Do you allow life to slip through your fingers while you sit around waiting for the past story to change its course of action?

When I got married, I was overjoyed. I felt like I was finally breaking the chains over my family. I was doing it the right way. As things started to unravel, communication halted, and I panicked. It was about over. I requested counseling – anything to hold on to the ideal. I said ideal because I knew that God did not put us together – we were unequally yoked. All the friends I had – we had seemed to disappear. I did not know who friend or foe was. Things got real right before our divorce. I got pregnant again. I was so distraught I considered getting rid of the child – despite my beliefs on abortion.

I ended up losing that child through miscarriage – crushing my heart again into a million pieces. Through all of that – I was eventually diagnosed with cancer from the miss-pregnancy. I knew then that the divorce was a moot point – I was now fighting for life. I went to the chemo treatments all alone – yet, somehow, I felt God's presence. I once broke down in the chemo room – it became too much. The nurses allowed me – their eyes told me I needed a good cry. For that moment, I was angry with God. How was I going to go through a divorce and chemo at the same time? I did not want to look at our pictures – our wedding attire. I felt lost. I started to believe that I was doomed to a life of failure. It seemed nobody understood – nowhere to turn, but then I realized I always had God. Then God spoke, and from that time on, I knew I would make it. He pulled my hands away, although often I was holding on tight. I wanted my life back – and my happy home – even if it was not real...

Free Indeed

Listen, My Friend, you are not the first to suffer, nor will you be the last. Take the lesson and run towards your future. Forgive yourself. When you can forgive yourself, you will find that you can forgive your others, too. Do not let the confusion of yesterday hinder your future.

Life is like a puzzle. We try to fit pieces into our lives that perhaps should never have been there or that clearly did not fit. Sometimes we are so determined to make them fit that we smash the pieces into the puzzle no matter how much distortion takes place. The good news is that God knows your puzzle. He knows what pieces belong where, and He surely knows how it is supposed to look. So, forgive what happened, and ask God to intricately place the pieces of your puzzle together. Doesn't that sound wonderful? Let God! God forgives us, even when we do not do things His way. His mercy picks us up where we are and stands us back up. The awesome thing is He does not go pointing fingers at us, like we often do to ourselves. He extends His grace and says, "Go forward now!" That is a miracle. It is time to stop pointing fingers at yourself or anybody else. History cannot be rewritten, but your future is a new chapter in which you can do things God's way. Allow yourself to be free: your freedom awaits you! You do not have to be a slave to your past any longer. The chains have been broken.

CHAINS

For many years I had thoughts toward writing this book. As I began to put those thoughts into actions, "chains" was the first word I visualized in my mind. Have you seen any strong chains lately? Businesses use them to keep trespassers out during the closed hours. People use chains to keep someone from stealing their bikes. The main purpose of chains is to keep someone or something out. Chains are most likely used to contain a prized possession – something of great value. As the thought of chains crept into my mind, I began to realize that the chains of life are *not* used to protect a prized possession, or to protect at all: they merely bind the person from growing, being fulfilled and being happy. The chains that most often are in our lives are the ones that keep us focused on what has happened in the past – the things that prevent us from living and connecting with people; they are the things that keep us from allowing anyone to get too close to us.

Chains come in many forms: grief, hatred, un-forgiveness, resentment, etc. but God's prized possession – that is you, My Friend – was not meant to be chained. You were meant to prosper, live abundantly, and walk into the future with joy. Chains do everything within their power as a stronghold to prevent that from happening. The chains in my life came in the form of poor self-acceptance – judging myself, not believing that I had anything to offer, and I did not know what it meant to tell people "no". I would avoid crowds – they just overwhelmed me. I did everything people asked – I wanted them happy even if I was not. I did many things that caused me anxiety. Forgetting my address at a conference - I was extremely nervous in the environment. Things have changed and I now can speak in front of people with confidence. (I am still working on the "no" part – it is a process). I believe that in order to overcome faith must be your guide. With faith you can do the impossible and move forward. I finally realized that God used a lot of creativity on me: for that I give thanks.

The truth, My Friend is that no matter how much those chains have caused you to believe that you must stay where you are - God broke those chains with great power and precision. When God breaks and releases the chains in your life, they do not just fall to the ground, My Friend: they vanish into nothingness! That which is ordered to flee, My Friend, will flee. Remove yourself from the prison that you have allowed yourself to wallow in. Find your freedom in God and in His glory. Your saying "yes" to yourself is exactly what you need. Every day we must rise and claim the freedom He so freely gives. God will show you how to have it. He never leaves you to do it on your own, because *"Greater is He that is in you, than he that is in the world."* (I John 4:4) Now that is truth - nothing but the truth

God Released

God released the chains from me.

Now I am living with peace - now I am free.

They had me bound and restricted,

Till God stepped in and said they had to be evicted.

In my mind they did not exist,

They were the ones I could not see with the naked eye.

God whispered, "It's not always the things you see: It's the things that set up camp on the inside.

Do you see the lie?"

God wrapped me in His arms and held me there.

All the protection I needed -held by His loving care.

God says His yoke is easy, and His burden's light.

He will fight your battles – give you reason for living.

He is the almighty Gift that keeps giving.

So, if you are tired of your chains, release the blame.

Open your heart to the heavenly Name.

Free Indeed

Jesus is the reason for every season.

He comes to bring forth hope, joy, peace, and love.

He is the Rock of all ages sent from above.

I promise you will never be the same,

Once you invite Him in to break the chain

You have the permission of God to let go and forgive everything that has been holding on to you. You must be willing to empty everything that does not belong - so that you can have room for what does. You might be saying that you want those who hurt you to pay for what they did. My Friend, your freedom is yours, and you are not free if you seek revenge. A vengeful heart is a chained heart. I held on for many years to pain as if it owned me – like it gave birth to me – I held it for dear life - only to realize I was holding my life back from so much more.

I had to learn to put on the full armor of God – the garments of wholeness, love, hope, forgiveness and the peace that it is well, no matter what the past consisted of. Be willing to decipher the lies you tell yourself. We often lie to ourselves because we have not opened the gift of truth. Our truth is in God. It is in the beauty of whom and how He made us. Allow that beauty of who you are to shine - so that not only the whole world will see the change, but so that you will see it, too. Forgive yourself for treating yourself less than worthy or beautiful. If you are a visual person like me, write your truth down and place it in your surroundings where you spend most of your time. Keep reminding yourself of whom and whose you are.

Make it your daily bread, My Friend. Sing to God, "Nobody loves me like you do!"

FEED ON THE WORD

One of the similarities that children have with one another is the song that they learned, "The B- I- B- L- E: now that's the book for me..." I can hear the children now yelling the word so loudly and forcefully. It was always a game at church camp to see who or which side of the building could scream the loudest. The adults always giggled at the fact that their ears seemed to be overpowered by those simple letters. The most powerful thing to note is that of all the books we pick up and read or pick up and put down - none of them has as much power and authority to change our life like the Bible does. It is the Book of books that has been around for an exceptionally long time, often collecting dust like a forgotten story. Every answer to life is collected in that Book, but we seldom consistently open it. Imagine what would happen if we would just take the time to allow the power that lies within that Book to flow into our lives and fill our souls!

Free Indeed

I have been a Christian since I was young, but the truth is I hardly ever read the Bible until later in my thirties. Astonishing right? Life happened, and I became so busy with living that the guidance and direction that waited within the Word sat somewhere hidden – unsought. God says that those who diligently seek Him will renew their strength. Wow! Seek Him? I sought friends and families when I was in need, but did I seek the Maker of all things? Did His forgiveness become my religion? Did I pick up His Word only when needed?

God wants us to come to Him, but He does not want us to come to Him only when we find ourselves trapped. Seeking Him means we sit with Him and talk and listen. He wants to fill you so that you thirst no more. He wants to breathe a new life into you, but it does take some willingness and effort on your part. So, wherever the B-I-B-L-E is in your home, take it out and become nurtured: you have starved for way too long.

I love to read, and whenever I read the Bible, I find something new in it. The word is refreshing every time, and it is so powerful that no Scripture can be read twice without out revealing more. God's message resonates through it, filling me with a truth greater than any that I have found in the world. What if we got excited like little children when we read the Book?

Have you ever looked up at the faces of children who are listening to someone read a book? Within their eyes there is expectation of what is going to happen, and smiles stretch their faces filling them with such excitement. They are honed onto every word. Some are on their knees; some are sitting Indian style. No matter the form, nothing can separate them from what they are hearing. They may giggle aloud or squirm where they sit, and you may even find one who wants to turn the page before it is time. What if we looked at the Bible with such delight – with anticipation of the news causing us to shift our position, heighten

the sensitivity of our ears to the words, and our hearts to beat in rhythm to the beat and glory of such a God? Can you imagine? Yet, we become complacent.

Don't you yearn for more? Draw nigh to Him: there is such a beautiful life in it! Let us live with hearts of the innocent that yearn for the touch of the Word, not hindered by the detours and the dry places of life. I often find myself shouting and praising Him while I read His word. I cannot contain myself, because that storage chest in which I hid the Bible for safekeeping has been opened – touching life brand new, sending shock waves through my body - and I shout, "Yes! Yes! It is mine! Everything that God has bestowed is mine - favored and blessed!" What about you?

Chapter Seven

Prayer Works

Getting into God's Word is so important: it is how He speaks to us. But do we ever speak back to Him? Often, we talk to everyone else, but we forget to talk to the most important person: God! I used to think that prayer required fancy rhetoric, big words and such. Can you imagine the man upstairs saying, "I can't hear you because you're not speaking my language"? I began to realize that God wants you to talk to Him just like He is one of your pals.

Having a conversation does not have to sound perfect. Speaking from your heart is the only requirement for communicating with the One who created you. No matter what life brings you, your connection with Him should become stronger, not weaker, even if you have moments (we all do) where your relationship is not where it should be. God does not require an Internet connection or a cell phone; to get in touch with Him does not require a pass code. Isn't that fantastic? How many of your friends, even your closest ones, are there whenever you call? I would bet that not many are. We all have lives and things that we are doing and taking care of, but God is never too busy. He is available 24/7, around the clock. If you feel disengaged, most likely it is not because *He* is not listening, but because *we* are not listening. I have spoken to God, even when the words would not form upon my lips. He hears the heart and sees the tears. He knows our queue. He is always in tune with his children – never forget that.

I just recently purchased a new printer – a very necessary tool for people who write. I got it for a steal – I love a good bargain. I brought it home and excitedly opened it. Now, I know you are thinking, "It's a printer lady!" Yes, I know, but now I have the capability to print out my works, whereas before, I dreaded library copy fees of 20 cents per page. (That might not seem like a lot but trust me: those cents start to add up). So, there I was placing the ink cartridges in their proper place; I plugged it in only to find out that I did not have a USB cable. The USB cable was not included. Kidding, right? Not at all! I never understood why it would not be included when something that is absolutely – without a shadow of doubt – considered necessary for something to work properly. It is beyond me. I mean, who thought of that? "Well, we are going to sell the printer, but we won't include the cords." It was a deal (but that surely is not my point). The point is my computer could not possibly communicate with the printer without the cord!

We are sometimes like that with God. It is God and us - but no prayer. You see where I am going? How can Christians become closer to their Creator if there is no communication? Have you ever shouted something to a friend who wasn't even with you? I am sure you would not. But if you did, would you expect them to hear you? No! If you want to say something to somebody that is not with you, most often you pick up the phone and call. God is forever with us, but we do not talk to Him, and we often tune out His voice. Raise your hand if you have done this. Come on do not be shy. My point is that we all have done this at one time or another. It is like we have cut the cord to the communication. God is still talking to us, but we cannot hear Him because we are walking in the flesh and not the Spirit.

Prayer is so important in a fruitful walk with God. He is your nudge when you are being stubborn and hardheaded. He is your peace in turmoil. He is your grace when you choose to do everything other than what you know to be right and true. He is everything, and He wants you in His presence. He wants to love on you. I have heard some very poetically spoken prayers. Have you ever heard a prayer spoken so eloquently that you think to yourself?

"Now there is no way I can top that"? Go ahead and giggle because we all have experienced that. God does not expect us to get out our best vocabulary, thesaurus, and dictionary to have a conversation with Him. Communication with Him requires *you*: your mind, body and spirit. He wants the genuine *you* to come at his feet and say, "Pops, I miss my time with you." No cool words, just a language straight from the heart. Our prayer life should be just as important as the food we eat, the jobs we go to or the time we spend with others. He is the One who said that all things are possible, so we need to make time for the Creator of time. Aren't you glad you do not need a USB cord to communicate with him?

PRAISE IS WHAT I DO

I give thanks to God for all that He has done and continues to do in my life. Without Him, where would I be? Through those valley and mountainous moments in life, God has been ever-present, even when I felt alone. I am not ashamed of Him or of my praise, because I know what could have become of me.

We all think that somehow our life trials and mishaps are the worst in the world. We try to compare them with this and with that. Honestly, they could always be worse. I have never slept in the car (unless, of course, I was traveling on a long journey and did not want to pay for a hotel). I am talking about being homeless – sleeping on a crushed box under a bridge. That could have been me. A humble reflection says I may have seen some rough times but thank God almighty I have not seen the worst of times. God has always made a way for me no matter what I was up against. He is the one constant factor in my life that has not changed. I have learned to count my blessings and trust me when I say there are plenty. So, praise is what I do. I praise with such an earnest heart, feeling His presence envelop me and bring me to a place of such peace.

Have you ever found yourself in such praise that you lift your hands right where you are with tears streaming down the check and dropping to the floor? Each tear that drops tells a story of "I made it!" It is when all the guards coming tumbling down and all that is left is a spirit that hungers for more of Him.

I love to sing - but singing was not the gift that God has given me. You cannot tell me that though, because when I am doing it, it is coming straight from the vessels of my heart. I bellow the song, a bit off-key, but it cleanses my soul, and I cannot quit. I am grateful, my Friend, to praise Him. It is the joy that flows like a mighty river out of the heart. When you do not know what to do, My Friend, just lift your hands and praise. Be grateful: it could have been you! When you take the focus off your problems you will realize that the tornado that tried to kill you did not. It is in your praise!

Praising does not mean just singing. Praise comes in many different forms. When I am at work, I think I am the only one who is smiling at my desk, saying "hello" with a joyful pitch. I catch myself smiling just thinking about the goodness of God in my life. When you have praise in your heart, people can see it in your behavior. They may wonder what you are so excited about. They did not know that God swells in your heart, and I could not hide it.

BROKEN BUT NOT DESTROYED

As humans we tend to treasure things: cell phones, iPods, computers, cars, etc. We even become attached to the people in our lives. We go out of our way to protect anything from happening to them. We treasure them because of the value that they hold. We know what it took for us to get them. We would rather not have a mishap because we just might not have any way to get them back. As human beings, we also become broken. When brokenness happens, most of us go into panic mode. We do not like change. We try to negotiate with God on what He has allowed to break. Surely, He would not take away those things which we hold so tightly or value so highly! So, we start giving God only the things we do not mind giving up. One thing is for sure: God gets His way. God does not break you, My Friend, because He wants to destroy you; He breaks you so that He can restore you. God is a perfecting God: good just is not good enough for Him. He will take your good, allow you to bask in it for a while, and then He will take it away. He knows when you have become comfortable. Comfortable often means you are not going any further; you stop growing.

When we find ourselves broken, we start asking, "Why?" Discouragement tries to slip in, and we start to grieve over the loss. God takes those broken pieces and forms something more beautiful than what we had before. He is a master artisan. His work is amazing! All who look at it are astonished. He sets the standard of great. If we would just stop being comfortable and allow God to work, we will find that which we lost was only for a time: God has some much bigger plans. My Friend I know it is hard to see the big picture right now, but if you will go the extra mile, you will find beauty awaiting you there.

A very incredibly special individual walked into my life one day. In the beginning I was a little hesitant to get to know him, so I just watched him closely. We eventually made a connection. We both are highly creative people. We seemed to complement one another. He opened a whole new way of thinking for me. What we had going on seemed like a dream-come-true! We became particularly good friends. And then, just as something was about to happen; we hit a fork in the road. I was so confused and did not understand what was happening. Suddenly, we started confusing one another. I found myself hurting and asking "Why?"

As I began to pray for understanding, something began to happen in me. (This is where you learn not to lean to your own understanding, but to trust God with all your heart, living expectantly that He will direct your paths.) I had some extremely hard moments, but I began to think of the greatness of God. His picture of greatness is so much grander than ours. I mean, we tend to stick to what we can see, touch or hear. God said that nothing is impossible to them who love Him. That became *my* truth, though many nights I wiped away tears. One of many faithful nights I told God, "I will trust you: I will let go of everything I think I have to hold onto." It is a small gesture of surrender. We become so used to making decisions and changing courses because it is what *we* want. What if we gave up what *we* want in order to get what *God* wants?

My Friend you may say, "How can I know what He wants?" I say, "Listen with your heart, mind and soul, and He will surely point the way." Do not be afraid to allow detours in your life: they are for your good. Why be disappointed, holding onto what you had, when you can be victorious by getting what He is giving? See, when you *look* up, My Friend, where you *go* is up. You have bigger thoughts, dreams, and aspirations for the impossible in your life. Who does not want that? You may ask me if I was ever afraid. Yes, I was, but fear is only a symptom of walking in the flesh, because the flesh tells us that good is good enough. I still find fear trying to take root in my life – trying to remind me of then. At those moments I must think on things of God. Whenever I found myself regressing into a pity party, I just said these four words, "Lord I trust you". When you speak that over yourself, you are putting Him in the driver's seat. You know, sometimes when we are in the driver's seat, we end up having accidents that could have been prevented. I would much rather have the comfort and security of having God as my driver. He never fails. My Friend are you ready to surrender the keys? If not, then listen to this story.

Once upon a time there was a monkey who saw something in a jar. It caught his eye, and he hurriedly rushed to the jar, heart pumping, and eyes dilated, and into the jar went his hand. He grabbed a hold of the object he had seen, tightened his little fist around it, and then he struggled and struggled to get his hand out of the jar. He tugged and pulled, firmly clasping in his hand what he so eagerly wanted to have. Time and time again he tried to break free, but to no avail. He sat there wondering to himself what he would do, for what he had in his hand was too good to let go of. He was trying to make sure that when his hand came out, he would have gotten what he went in for. After many unsuccessful attempts, he finally realized that it was more important to be free than to be trapped holding onto something he could not have.

"God, please teach us the lesson of the monkey, and help us release everything that is not for us, so that we may walk toward what is."

My Friend, you may be broken, but be beautifully broken, and move toward your healed self.

Beautifully Broken

Broken like glass into many pieces…

God, I did not realize you were molding me-

Taking pieces, forming, changing - stretching the core of my soul.

Broken of the flesh; that is what it took my spirit to become whole.

I thought I had everything I needed to survive.

Then you taught me in God I thrive not just survive I must have been asleep, in too deep to understand the meaning. I hear you; ears up close, conversation so good – I am not leaving. They say broken is destroyed; He says that broken is beautiful.

Waste nothing: He is the master Artisan, creating and using me.

He sees where I am going, not where I am.

In my brokenness is where Jesus is found.

Chapter Eight

Gratefulness

I am so big on gratefulness that it really gets under my skin when my children forget to say, "thank you". I constantly remind them of the importance of showing gratitude. Certainly, times have changed, and many of the youth today have the idea that life owes them something – partly because they are used to getting everything. We pamper them so much that they have no use for gratefulness, because life becomes an entitlement. They see life through the eyes of self. I grew up with extraordinarily little. Game systems were a luxury. Having anything that was mine and mine alone was a rarity. We shared everything: the bed, our clothing, our toys… It was the life of "what's mine is yours", and vice versa, and we were all happy. I was grateful that God gave me a grandmother who had the capability to raise her daughter's children. I was grateful God got me through some truly trying times while others succumbed. I was grateful God instilled within me such passion to help people and to be humble.

Free Indeed

When you can give thanks even for the small things, God will trust you with so much more. Never become so proud that you cannot even see the blessing in the lessons. Open your eyes so that you can see the purpose of the lessons. Sometimes we forget to give God thanks for waking us up another day and guiding us through our day. We get arrogant and angry, blaming God for what *is not* happening rather than thanking for Him for what *is* happening. If you are breathing, be thankful. You have been given another moment to pursue your purpose with passion.

Be thankful for the people who cared enough to let you go so that you can be blessed with God's best. It stops you from walking around mad: instead - glad that God is still working on your behalf.

I am forever grateful that God has strengthened me to raise my children to be strong individuals. He has allowed me to be an example for them to persevere. He kept my mind, spirit and heart so that I may do the job He has called me to do. My Friend let us get an attitude of gratitude for all things. There is a reason for every season and purpose revealed. Let us not get so stuck in the details that we miss the lesson. It is our lesson that boosts our zeal to carry on. It will be the thrust you need to get you from where you are to where you are going. Be grateful.

<u>RELEASING YOURSELF FROM THEIR VIEW OF YOU</u>

The Chains That Love Broke

We live in an instant world with instant pictures and instant messages. We get everything in a hurry. We take pictures of ourselves everywhere we go; in the bathroom, in public, at church... Every place becomes fair game. Of all the pictures we take, we always post the best ones, because some of them just show too many of our faults. We look at every single blemish and we tell ourselves things like, "I'm too fat", "I'm too skinny", "I'm too short", "I'm too tall", or, "I'm not smart enough". We describe ourselves in ways that are less than beautiful; rather seeing ourselves the way God see us. We are not satisfied. We want to be like somebody else – their looks, their intelligence, their life – viewing their life as better than ours.

God created you. No two things are the same: no two birds, no two trees, and no two people. We are unique and created by the hands of beauty. When we begin to see ourselves in the spiritual realm, our physical self will align with it as well. We are so hard on ourselves because we believe somehow that if we were not who we are, then we would be better accepted, and maybe people would treat us right instead of walking out of our lives. We fool ourselves into believing that if there were something different – something better – about us, then it would affect who others are and how they relate to us. We play the game of "all I have to do is change me, and the world will change with me." Listen, My Friend, I do not care if you are the queen or the president, people are still going to be people. Jesus was who He was, and did that make everybody like him? No. In fact, they hated Him so much that they crucified Him. He was love – He spoke it, He lived it – and yet He still had enemies. He was the epitome of beauty, yet people did ugly things to Him. What makes you any different? They mocked everything that He stood for, spat on Him and nailed His hands to a cross. Just imagine Jesus on that cross saying, "Please, people, if you would just let me off this cross, I will denounce who I am, and I promise to become just like you people who have me hanging here." But instead of blaming Himself there on the cross, He looked up to His Heavenly Father and said, "God forgive them, for they know not what they do." He still showed love, and He embraced who He was, even though He knew that the people who put Him there hated everything He stood for.

My Friend, there are going to be people who hate everything you stand for – they won't even like your looks – and there is nothing you can do to yourself or by yourself that can make each and every person who crosses your path like you. The person that needs to accept you - is *you*. God accepts everything about you because He created you in His image. He did not make you in the image of someone else, but in *His* image. If God was pleased with His work, then you, too, can be pleased with His work. We must learn to stop knocking ourselves down: there are already too many people who will do that for you. If nobody else cherishes you, My Friend, cherish yourself. Show yourself unconditional love, because if *you* cannot show yourself love, then how on earth can you expect anyone else to?

There was a time when I was responding to a post about relationships on another person's FB page, and there was a lady who said that she was too damaged – that no man would ever want her, and that she just had to be happy with the fact that she had children who loved her. I read this, and I thought to myself, "How disappointed God must be that we would see ourselves in such a manner." God made each person, and He never, ever says that it is too late for any of us. Cutting the cord of doom and pity must happen. My Friend you going to put away those self-inflicting hurtful words, and we are going to replace them with love and acceptance for yourself and for the God who created you. My Friend do whatever it takes to change your mind today. You are beautiful by God's standard, not the standard set by men. You are priceless, irreplaceable and never duplicated. You are "one in infinity" because "one in a million" still allows a chance that there is another you. God's creative ability does not end at a million. His creativity is endless: He does not run out of ideas or possibilities, and He does not have to have an eraser, because He always gets it right the first time.

SHUTTING THE DOOR

When it is all said and done, we must come to the realization that we need to once-and-for-all shut the door to everything that *was*. There is a huge price that we pay for allowing the past to continue releasing poison into our future. God wants to see His people prosper, and you cannot prosper with your back turned to your future. There is so much that awaits you there and God is so ready to guide you; together. Begin to prioritize the things that you can change in the here and now. If it were possible to erase the past, most of us would, My Friend, but the reality is *it is not*. Even when Jesus has broken the chains of our past, we often pick up the chain's pieces – as if they were tokens or prized possessions. I want to encourage you to look ahead: with your lessons and strength gained, so much awaits you! It may mean that you must shut the door to old ways of thinking, ways of believing, people's ways, and the likes. This new chapter of your life comes already transformed. Just think of all the times life has brought change to you. Didn't God help you? Didn't you make it through? This time in your life is no different: you will make it through this as well. Our view is often so shortsighted. We forget that we have overcome a lot. The fact that some doors are closing also means that some new ones are being opened for you and that you will forge for yourself a better way of existing. Look forward to what is to come. Opening new chapters should be an exciting time.

In order to arrive at the meat of a book it takes going through layers and layers of stories. What if the meat or the heart of your story was at the beginning (or in the middle for that matter)? If everything great has already happened, could you be excited about the future? I believe that God's intentions are for us to move from good to better to best. The door that closed may have been good, but do not settle for good. Imagine the most impossible hope or dream and imagine a God so big and magnificent that you will probably never utterly understand the magnitude of it all. A closed door should be viewed at as an opportunity to touch His promises for you. I will bet you could get excited about that! Every time one road ends, there is always an adjoining road that takes you to the next path. Sometimes we become too accustomed to that road. We become so fixated on how something looks, feels or smells that we cannot even glance in the direction of the new that God is trying to give us. For every road that ends there is a newness that begins. We must allow ourselves to be pulled away from what we have become attached to and what we want in order to get what we need.

I like the idea of "Perfectly Human" we want to be the actors, and the directors. We like to know what we are going to be doing, how we are going to do it and whom we are going to do it with. We become uncomfortable when things begin to look different than the way we planned them. Isn't it ironic that sometimes the things we plan become everything that we do not need? Could it mean that we do not always know what is best for us? But that never stops us from trying. God does know what is best for us, and it is high time that we let Him do what He knows we need and what is best for us. Yes, new things bring a little discomfort to us, but staying where we are will bring an even greater discomfort. Little babies love their toys, but they will drop that toy they adored so much once they lay eyes on the new, shiny thing that has been introduced to them. They are always willing to try something different. They explore their environment with little or no reluctance.

You must learn to explore again. Such a vast world as the one God has given you to live in is worth exploring. Once you get over the initial shock of the unfamiliar, God can show you everything He wants you to have. You must be willing to seek His face and allow Him to direct your paths. His wisdom is much greater than man's wisdom, so let Him pave the path that He want you to take. You must allow Him to reposition you so that you will be set towards your destiny and not turned away from it.

Chapter Nine

You Matter

When God is the One Who chooses your course in life, He will make sure that you are well-cared for. In a terribly busy fast-paced world, the person who most often takes the back seat to everything is us. We do not know ourselves, our likes, our dislikes or our boundaries. We commit to everything and everyone, but we do not commit to taking care of someone particularly important; us! What is it that you like? What is it that you want? It is not selfish to take care of yourself or love yourself, My Friend. For you to be able to give to others, you must first have what you are trying to give. You cannot love others without loving yourself. You cannot give of yourself if you do not know who you are. We become like water flowing in every direction except in the direction God has called us to.

There is nothing wrong in giving, My Friend. In fact, God expects you to give. You cannot give, My Friend, if you are running on empty. It is Ok to stop and say "no" to something that is making you uncomfortable. Say "no" to things that have you compromising who you are and what you stand for. Everything that we do, and touch should exemplify our God. It should not drain us, change who we are, or compel us to do things that are outside of our best self. I often found myself reaching out to help everybody with their problems, but I was not helping myself. I ran to the rescue of all who called - often at a detriment to myself. I did things and said things that seemed pleasing to others, but was I being myself?

If you must be anybody other than yourself to accomplish what you want to accomplish, then it is not a goal God has established for you. Healed people heal people. Find what it is that you want, My Friend. What makes you happy? What brings you peace of mind and vitality to thrive – not just survive? Do you give to receive because you feel that you are lacking, or do you give because God has filled you with an overflow and you have enough to go around? See, whatever you do should be done with God-centeredness that says, "I know who I am in God, and those who come across my path will see Him in me, too." What is the common ingredient that you need in order to drive a car, fly a plane, or heat your home? You need gas; without fuel none of those items will run. You can put your key in the ignition, but if there is no gas; you will not get far. The fumes may take you down the street, but eventually you will be stranded.

Would you get on a plane without proper fuel? I would surely hope not. In the winter months do you neglect to pay your heating bill in hopes that the gas company will not notice? It would be a very cold winter if you did this. My point is that *you*, My Friend, cannot run on empty. Let God's love fill you to an overflowing capacity so that not only will you keep going, but you will also have plenty to share with the stranded. During this journey of life, do not forget the gifts and the talents that God has bestowed upon you: they are meant for your use. It is ok to take care of everybody else, but you, too, are important.

God made me a highly creative person. I love art, music and writing, but these are things that got thrown to the wayside as I became less important to me. I began to do the things that brought other people's hopes and dreams to fruition, but not my own. There was no *me* in the things that I was doing because I thought that was what I was supposed to do. When the chips started to fall, I was left wondering what I was going to do. My life had become their life. I no longer knew who I was. So, when I was left alone, I was like a lost child who could not find my way. I became frustrated because my happiness consisted of others. They were my life. Remember to never lose sight of who you are, because you are the person that you also need. You rely on you. You depend on you. If you are not strong enough to depend on you, then you cannot expect anyone else to.

Free Indeed

My sister use to get to go everywhere when we were little. I remember being told, "You can't come because you're too little." Now when I hear "you're too little," my brain says, "Wait a minute: she is only a year older than I am." It was complete injustice in my mind, but I would watch her and her friends trail away, and I would just stomp off and go get on my Big Wheel and ride like the wind till my heart was content. I rode up and down that street so much that I think I knew how many blocks of cement there were, or how many cracks were in them.

There will be times, My Friend, when you will have to leave some folks behind. I know you have been best buds, road dogs, or whatever you want to call it. You will never stop growing in life, especially when you live in the will of God. There will be shifts in each season of your life, and sometimes that means you also will have to shed some things and some people. We get used to people that we have known many years and have grown up with, and that is ok. But when God wants to do certain things in your life, sometimes it is just meant for you, My Friend. You may outgrow some people so that you can grow into who God wants you to be. Either they will understand, or they will stay behind. Growth cannot be hindered by your inability to change with the seasons and your unwillingness to walk into your seasons by yourself. Some people hold onto things and people – not out of necessity, but because they feel like they need to bring their own cheerleaders and backbone. My Friend, God already knows what you need and when you need it. He has already positioned in place everything and everybody you need through your next chapter. So, what if so-and-so does not like it? This season is not about them, but about you. You cannot go the speed you need to go to riding with folks who are still in training wheels. Those on training wheels are going to slow you down, and if they want to ride with you then they are going to have to grow with you or they cannot go with you.

My Friend, we must get to the point where we trust God and everything that He is bringing us to and through. Your blessings and lessons are not for everybody, My Friend. Do not halt God's plan for your life, My Friend, because you cannot see it fully. Your God is bigger than any box that you can put Him in. You can try and stuff him a small box, but I assure you it is not going to happen. Eagles, unlike many birds, fly alone. They fly high above the clouds and they soar. They do not follow the crowd; they do not try and be something they are not. They are revered for who they are and what they stand for.

PURPOSE

What are you on this earth for? That is your purpose. I have had many jobs to bring money into the home. They were not what God intended for me, but sometimes we do what is not intended before we arrive at our purpose. As I child I always knew that God had something special in mind for me. Throughout my many endeavors I always felt a calling on my life. This, at times, intimidated me because I often felt unworthy of this calling. God does not call his children out because they are better than the next person or because they have not done things that were displeasing to Him. Purpose means that what God has called you to do is not meant for anybody else but you. God needed *your* personality; *you are* thinking capacity and *your* gifts, to do the job He needs you to do. If it were left up to anybody else it just would not be the same, because your purpose was designed with *you* in mind. Anybody else would just be a copycat.

I knew that God was calling me into ministry and believe me; I did anything and everything to avoid that call on my life. I made a lot of noise in my life to keep from abiding and obeying the call. I was miserable doing it, too. When you have been called to do the will of God, you will be nothing but restless doing anything else. I would find myself saying, "God, you really want me to minister to people? Are you sure? Isn't someone else better equipped with higher qualifications and degrees?" When God places you in the line of service, there is nothing that can stop it from coming full force. It will happen regardless of your education, your past, your qualifications or your resume. When God places a promise over your life it becomes reality regardless of what anyone else says. In fact, everything that you have been through and come through has prepared you for the next phase of your life. It was everything you needed that pressed you into who you are now. You have everything inside you that you need in order to do God's will and excel at it. Believe in your call and in your God.

God uses some of the most unlikely people to do His greatest work. Romans 9:17 says, *"I raised you up for this reason so that I may display my power in you and that my name may be proclaimed in all of the earth."* Your own human will, or capacity is not what matters here: it is the work that God is doing in you. It is His compassion and mercy over you that allow you to walk out your purpose. In His perfection you are perfected.

FROM PAST TO PROMISE

God is calling you out of your rut – the past that has you tangled in its web. It is time for you to wake up and see what is before you and for you. All that you have been through has not stopped your destiny. What you need right now is to love of yourself unconditionally: accept and acknowledge who you are and whose you are. You do not have to wait for the chains to be broken, My Friend, they are already broken. You are free to walk ahead into your destiny. God has opened the door of freedom than no man can shut. In Christ you are a new person with new thoughts, and behaviors. You do not talk like you used to talk, your walk is different, and your love is different. People are trying to figure you out because they do not know you anymore. Something has changed. God has changed you so that you will know that it is His working through you that makes all the difference in the world.

Remind yourself not to sacrifice your destiny ever again because of your past. You are God's chosen, incredibly loved and holy. You must learn to see what He sees in you and walk in compassion, kindness, humility and patience. You owe this to others and to yourself.

HOW MUCH MORE

My Friend, how much more time will you give to your past? Time waits for no one; neither does time have time for things that are already done. Have you ever been sitting at a four-way cross, and everybody is just sitting waiting for someone to take the initiative to pass so that everyone else can get to where they are going? And then, just when one person decides they are going to go, someone else starts to move at the same time? Eventually things start to move in the right direction. Life is like that, too. Sometimes things need to pass, but we keep it from doing so. We get in the way of its passing.

We must refuse to be stuck at a four way stop. You may have some tough decisions to make on this journey, but with clarity from God and your strength to proceed, you will get that which no longer matters to move past and away from you. You do not have to wait for your past to give you permission to let it go.

Only you have the control and power to say, "Be moved from me." Each new day breeds hope, and newness of life and the opportunities therein, but if your yesterdays are still crowding your tomorrows – there is still much work to do. Do not give what was (or what could have been) to what *is* and what *will be.* Your promise is in your today and your tomorrow. God cannot bless your yesterday, My Friend, but what He can bless He will, and you just must see with the spiritual eyes that are within you. My Friend you are standing in front of two doors: one has your past in it, and the other holds your promises of greatness, happiness, joy, peace, and love. Which will you choose? If you choose the first one, you will lose your future, but if you choose the door God has created for you, it places you in a winning atmosphere. I am not saying that along the way there will not be other battles, but what I am saying is that the God Who goes before you have already won them all. With grace you overcome, and with purpose you step out to do the things that God has created you to do. You cannot straddle the fence and expect the blessing to reveal itself. Revelation comes when you allow God to be God in and through your life. *In* you He strengthens; *through* you He reveals. How much are you willing to gamble on God's investment in you? Would you go and buy stock that has already crashed? I would surely hope not. So why do you keep investing in things that happened yesterday when the only return you will get is more hindrance of your tomorrow? God invested in you because He knows His creation. He knows what would happen if you would break out of the chains that keep you bound. He knows the greatness that lies within. He knows the purpose that He has blessed in your life. He is just waiting for you to see it.

Chapter Ten

Shoes That Fit

When growth happens, you outgrow some things. When you have outgrown a pair of shoes, would you continue to wear them, or would you purchase some new ones? I could only imagine how miserable you and your feet would be if you kept wearing those too-small shoes while trying to do what needs to get done. You would walk around limping, whining, complaining and being irritated and unpleasant. People would not care to be around a person with an unpleasant attitude. Why should they let you cramp their style because you are wearing shoes that have cramped yours?

Honestly, I am not really talking about shoes, but I am talking about letting things cramp your style – walking around mad at the world, complaining about this and that, because the situation you have found yourself in is uncomfortable. Do you realize that you are uncomfortable because growing *is* uncomfortable at times? You are merely having growing pains because what God wants to grow in you is not finding the space to flourish: you are still holding on to what was meant to go. Throw it away, My Friend. Let it, them, they, whatever, and whomever, go. It is time for you to walk comfortably in your own size. Break out of the things that do not fit into your life or your destiny. Yes, it may be uncomfortable, but pleasantry is not going to come if you do not break out. Your attachment to those things that no longer fit will deprive you of your destiny.

Do not go on a starvation diet, trying to fit into the old you. Feed on the promises of God, and that which you thought you needed, will become an afterthought. Don't you want to try on things that have been created with *you* in mind? Don't you want all that has been custom-made for you? The right people, the right thoughts and right living will find you - but you must find the God in you first. You may have covered yourself with so much of a mess that it seems you cannot emerge but trust me: you can with the help of God. Emerge to a happier, healthier you. You will become someone who is not held back by back *then*: someone who is living in the grace of what *is*.

I once wore shoes that did not fit me, and I was not being myself. I was trying to make the uncomfortable more comfortable. I tried to fit in with people in places that were not the right place for me to be. I wanted it (so I thought) because being somewhat included felt better than walking alone most times. But finally, I realized that God does not want me to fit in: He wants someone who can go about His business with a boldness to say, "The God in me fits perfectly; therefore, I can fit perfectly in whom He created me to be." I began to understand that I needed to be able to walk in authority, but I could not do it when I was wearing shoes that were not for me. I learned to embrace who I was fully and completely.

THE BEST IS YET TO COME

There is nothing like an intriguing book that grabs your attention as you hold it - mesmerized by the words on the printed page – taking your mind to far-away places. The first part of a book that catches my eye is the title. It gives me just a small inkling of the story that is inside. I reach for it, flipping through the pages with interest. I read the first few lines looking for the engagement that perhaps will interest me enough to purchase it. I always read while I wait. A week ago, I had an appointment which I knew would take me an exceptionally long time. I always prepare myself when I have an appointment of some sort that I anticipate will last a few hours: I carry a book or headphones for my musical enjoyment. I pick up one of many books at my disposal that I have yet to read and my cell phone fully charged and ready with headphones. I sit comfortably in my seat with book in hand, while others talk among themselves or stare into space. Once there was a lady sitting next to me. Her continual gaze pierced through me with such intensity that it began to make me a little nervous. I could not understand what interested her so. That nervousness subsided when I realized that what I was reading was so powerful to me! I realized that just maybe, in the brief time she had, she could grasp a few parts of it. It could be something she needed in her own life. I began to relax, and I read the whole book by the time my appointment was finished. I recall leaving the book on the chair while I went to take a restroom break, only to return to a conversation brought on by the man who sat on the other side of me. The title had also grabbed his attention, and he wanted to know more about it. He even encouraged me to share it with the whole room. Of course, sharing it was not possible, but it was a cute thought. Your life is a book, and every day it gets written in, creating such astonishing, creative stories. (I know you are probably wondering where I am going with this.) What keeps us turning the page in our life? It is the drive to get better – to see each chapter through with a courageous heart. But what if the best part of your story was at the beginning or in the middle? What if it was boring? Would a book that does not get better be a true reflection of the powerful God we serve? Would you be excited about turning the page? I would think not, and that book may find itself collecting cobwebs or being overpowered by more interesting books.

When I reflect on the magnitude of God, it reminds me that a book entwined with such grandeur cannot ever possibly be ineffective or boring. What keeps people looking over your shoulder to see what is next? You are not just any ordinary book, but a book that has the special signature of your Heavenly Father! It is never duplicated or bland. He is the most creative Being known to man, and His work of art is inspiring to those who see it. God keeps it interesting; He keeps all who read wanting more and craving what is inside. Your life book serves as testimony to others. The best is yet to come! God can never be outdone, so as long we grace this earth, our lives can only get better. If your life book keeps it interesting - thank God! What is your book's title? What is it saying about your God? You must be excited about each new chapter. A story full of God's wonder is one book that no one will ever want to put down. The best is yet to come! Create your expectancy by turning the next page.

Grasp your bundle of peace, joy, hope and love and hold it close: it is your baby. You need to release your inner happiness into the world and vow never, ever to allow your circumstances and situations to darken your light, My Friend. God has given you every power and authority to rise above and be all that He has created you to be. You are blessed beyond measure. You are blessed coming in and blessed going out. Nothing that has happened to you can hinder you unless you allow it. Give every care to Him who loves you unconditionally. You are special, and you are God's gift to the world.

Others may have done you wrong and mistreated you, but you were merely being cut and polished, and now you are a diamond. Yes, it may have took some time to see just whose and who you are, but what is more important is that now you can see the Light, and that Light will shine through you. God is going to take your little bit and make it much. You made it out of the lion's den untouched, and you have a testimony that will change the world for the better!

Do not be afraid to live courageously and abundantly. If God be for you, who can be against you? Every day God gives you the promise that you will walk in your faith and Truth. You will proclaim who is Lord of your life. He says that you are the head and not the tail! Do you believe that? Be like David and go into your future courageously – not because you can see the path clearly, but because you put your trust in the One Who does. He will see you through it, and you will come out glistening. God's promises to you and for you will never return to Him void. He does what He says He will do regardless of what you see in the physical.

Our eyes fool us sometimes, we must put on our spiritual eyes that God has equipped us with - nothing on this green earth shall blind his truth again. Nothing that is revealed and clear to God can stay covered. We live and walk by faith, not by sight. We serve the most powerful God, and nothing and no one can ever come close to such magnificent power. It is mind-blowing – earth shattering – and the devil trembles at His sight. The devil may have convinced you in the past that you are messed up, broke up, and worthless, but God made a liar out of him when He rescued you from the den, My Friend. He heard you all along – even when you thought you were alone. You were not. In fact, when you thought you were in it alone and could not walk another step is when He picked you up in his loving arms and carried you. Can you trust Him to take you to the next level? Don't you have enough evidence that He is who He says He is?

Why do not you take a moment right now – right where you are – *and settle this matter once and for all, My Friend? Right now, just look to your Heavenly Father and say,* "I know things have not always went the way I desired, there were times circumstances seemed to weigh me down. I did not always listen to your voice and I made some choices that were not always your best plan for me. And right now, I want to forgive myself and others. Father, I ask that you reveal yourself within me. I release myself from all feelings of guilt of what happened, and I choose, from this moment forward, to live in the power and freedom of my all-powerful God, not in the chains of my past or circumstances. Father, I accept your love for me – all of me – and I ask you to help me learn to accept myself. Fill me with your love and acceptance so that I can give it out to others who need it as well.

Use me for your glory. I want to shine with the Light of Jesus who lives in me. The past is past. A glorious future awaits, and I want to rejoice in the victory that you offer me today. Thank You, Jesus, for making this all possible! Amen."

Conclusion

My Friend, you can wake up every morning and rejoice that you are no longer a slave to your past. Your mind can be renewed by the Word of God, and your spirit can be refreshed and invigorated by basking in His presence. Healing takes your willing participation – our action moves God to action. Those chains that once bound you are now broken. Let them go. Do not stoop to pick up even one little piece of them. They are dead weight. God has something far, far better for you to wear! It is not that you have forgotten, but that you have let go. God does not tell the story of the beginning by its end. Far greater is before than what is behind. Go forth in strength and victory – greater is your strength that is found in our Lord and Savior Jesus Christ. May you be blessed forever more!

My Friend, I have held your hand – we have pulled up some weeds. I know it was not easy, and I know it was hard. The work that is often needed is going to be hard, but you deserve to be free. It will take your being patient with you and leaning on God when you feel like you cannot go another mile. You have come this far, and I believe you will go even further. You *can* do it and I

know you will. See you on the road of total healing! You are free –
it is finished

Kimberlee O. is the mother of three wonderful children – a boy and two girls. They are her joy in life! She earned her bachelor's degree in Psychology in 2011. She currently lives in Southern U.S.A, with her two daughters. She enjoys reading, drawing, painting and writing.

For many years, Kimberlee's dreams sat dormant - hidden within her heart. But now through her writing, painting and preaching she shares a vivid testimony of the mighty God she serves and the grace and mercy that He continues to show to them that love Him. She uses her gifts to testify to others that no matter the circumstance – God is still God, and He never, ever fails!

Kimberlee does want to be viewed as the one who "went through" She prefers to describe herself as on who has an incredible desire and ability to take her broken pieces and allow God to turn them into masterpieces. She invites you into her journey so that you, too, may find the warrior within and conquer. Her dream is that through her story, *The Chains That Love Broke,* others will find that the chains they thought held them bound have been broken by the blood of Jesus!

www.ingramcontent.com/pod-product-compliance
Lightning Source LLC
Chambersburg PA
CBHW072041040426
42447CB00012BB/2958